AMERICA GOES TO WAR

WORLD WAR II
IN THE PACIFIC
TIMELINES, FACTS, AND BATTLES

By Craig Boutland

Published in 2023 by The Rosen Publishing Group, Inc.
2544 Clinton Street, Buffalo, NY 14224

Editor: Lindsey Lowe
Children's Publisher: Anne O'Daly
Design Manager: Keith Davis
Picture Manager: Sophie Mortimer

Picture Credits:
Front Cover:Public Domain
t = top, b = bottom, c = center
Alamy: PJF Military Collection 26, UtCon Collection 42t; Imperial War Museum: 48-49c, 48-49b, 49t; Lebrecht Collection: 10, 12t; Pubic Domain: AFP/Stringer/ibtimes 61b, Bettmann 9t, ibiblio.org 42-43b, IJN 31t, Ministry of Defence of the Russian Federation 54, 54-55, 55c, PRC 48t, PRC/sina.com 55t; Robert Hunt Library: 5, 6, 8, 9b, 16, 17, 18, 19, 20, 21, 28, 29, 32, 34, 35t, 35b, 38, 40, 41, 44, 45, 47, 50, 51, 52, 53, 56, 57, 58t, 59; Shutterstock: Everett Collection: 39, 58b; TopFoto: 12b; United States Government: Department of Defense/ibiblio.org 60t, NARA 14-15, 15t, 24t, 25t, 36c, 43c, 48b, 61c, Signal Corp Photo 61t, U.S. Army 25b, 60b, U.S. Navy 14t, 24b, 30, 30-31c, 30-31, 36t, 36-37b, Naval History and Heritage Command 36-37c, 37t, 37b, 43t, U.S. War Department 49b.

Cataloging-in-Publication Data

Names: Boutland, Craig.
Title: World War II in the Pacific: timelines, facts, and battles / Craig Boutland.
Description: New York : Rosen Publishing, 2023. | Series: America goes to war| Includes bibliographic references, index and glossary.
Identifiers: ISBN 9781499474008 (pbk) | ISBN 9781499474015 (library bound) | ISBN 9781499474022 (ebook)
Subjects: LCSH: World War, 1935-1945—Pacific Area —Juvenile literature
Classification: LCC D767 B68 2023 | DDC 940.54/26—dc23

Manufactured in the United States of America

CPSIA Compliance Information: Batch #CWRYA23. For further information contact Rosen Publishing at 1-800-237-9932.

 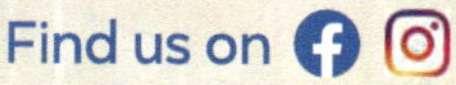

CONTENTS

Introduction

World War II was the largest and most destructive war in history. Between 1939 and 1945, 100 million troops were mobilized across the world.

In the Pacific, the war ranged from naval battles fought by aircraft flying from carriers that never came within sight of one another to fierce hand-to-hand fighting on the coral islands.

The Course of the War

Japan sought to expand in Southeast Asia to secure supplies of resources such as oil. Its best chance of victory was to knock out the United States before its superior industrial strength could have an impact. The Japanese air strike on Pearl Harbor, Hawaii, in December 1941 achieved complete surprise but failed to strike the decisive blow. Still, Japan's initial advance swept aside Allied resistance and brought much of Southeast Asia under Japanese command, from Burma to the Philippines. The United States was rebuilding its fleet strength, however, and, in a series of naval clashes, won an advantage over the Japanese. That allowed U.S. planners to launch thrusts from island to island across the vast ocean. As U.S. marines made a series of difficult amphibious landings, a combination of aircraft carriers and captured airbases brought U.S. forces within striking distance of Japan itself. Stiff Japanese resistance in the island campaign eventually convinced the U.S. leadership to use the new atomic bomb rather than risk a conventional landing on the home islands.

About This Book

This book focuses on the war in the Pacific from 1941 to 1945. It contains two types of timelines. Along the bottom of the pages is a timeline that covers the whole period. It lists key events and developments, including from Europe and North Africa, color coded. Each chapter also has its own timeline, which runs vertically down the sides of the pages. This timeline gives more specific details about the particular subject of the chapter. IN FOCUS spreads give more detailed information on personalities, battles, and weapons.

U.S. Marines wade ashore from a landing craft in the invasion of Guadalcanal, in the Solomon Islands, in August 1942.

The Approach of War

The Japanese attack on Pearl Harbor on December 7, 1941, stunned the world. In fact, the storm clouds of war had been gathering over the Pacific for two decades.

Japanese troops head to China in the 1930s. The Japanese invaded northern China in 1931.

TIMELINE **1941 NOVEMBER–DECEMBER**

KEY: Pacific | Eastern Front | Europe and North Africa

November 26 Pacific Ocean
Japanese aircraft carriers set sail for Pearl Harbor, Hawaii. The aim is to destroy U.S. warships in the region and then to seize land in the Pacific and Asia.

November

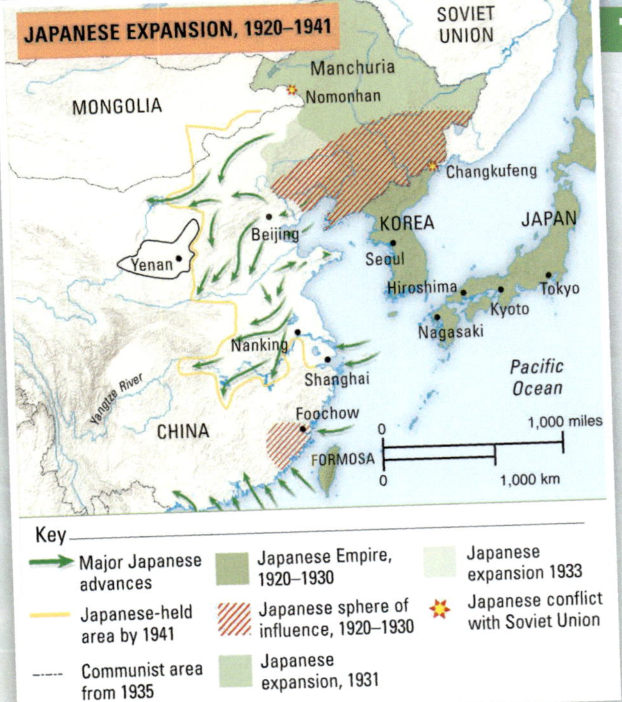

← Territorial expansion was a key part of Japan's long-term modernization.

Japan's modernization began in 1867. The Meiji Restoration brought the emperors back to power and ended a period of 250 years of international isolation.

Japan had joined the Allies (Britain, France, and the United States) in World War I (1914–1918). After Allied victory, however, the peace settlements forced Japan to give up the Chinese territory it had conquered.

KEY DATES

1922 Washington Naval Treaty restricts Japan's naval power in the Pacific.

1924 U.S. Immigration Act stops Japanese immigration to the United States.

1926 Pro-Western Emperor Hirohito comes to the Japanese throne.

1931 Imperial Japanese Army invades Manchuria.

1932 Japan rejects the Washington Naval Treaty.

1933 Japan withdraws from the League of Nations.

1936 Japan negotiates Anti-Comintern Pact with Germany.

July 1937 Start of second Sino-Japanese War.

December 1937 Japanese aircraft sink USS *Panay*.

December

December 7 Hawaii
Some 183 Japanese aircraft attack the U.S. Pacific Fleet at Pearl Harbor. They destroy 16 ships and 188 aircraft, damage or sink 10 other vessels, and kill 2,000 people.

December 8 Soviet Union
Adolf Hitler halts the German advance on Moscow for the winter.

December 8 United States
The United States declares war on Japan.

December 10 Pacific Ocean
About 90 Japanese aircraft sink two British warships, *Prince of Wales* and *Repulse*, with the loss of 730 sailors.

The Kwantung Army

The Kwantung Army, also known as the Guandong Army, was originally a small garrison stationed in Manchuria, northern China, to defend Japan's commercial interests. In 1931, operating without government approval, the Japanese army's commanders faked a bombing on a train and occupied all of Manchuria. The army remained in northern China until the end of World War II, rising to a peak strength of around 700,000 men. It finally surrendered after a Soviet offensive in August 1945.

→ Students undergo military training in the 1930s with guns that only fire blanks.

A later agreement limited the size of Japan's navy in the Pacific. The Japanese believed their former allies were now treating them like a second-class nation. The Japanese also resented the Western powers' Asian colonies. Japan had to import nearly all of its food, metal, and oil. It wanted its own colonies to provide such goods. Prejudice against Japanese immigrants on the U.S. West Coast was another cause of tension between Japan and the United States.

Many conservatives resented what they saw as Japan's humiliation. They argued Japan should look to traditional values, such as those followed by Japan's warriors, the samurai.

Hard-Liners Take Control

As militaristic views grew more popular, the Japanese army increasingly acted outside government control. It invaded Manchuria in northern China in 1931 (see sidebar, left).

TIMELINE **1942 JANUARY–FEBRUARY**

KEY:  **Pacific** **Eastern Front** **Europe and North Africa**

January

January 5 Soviet Union
Stalin's troops counterattack; their initial success halts as the Germans set up defenses.

January 10–11 Dutch East Indies
Japanese troops attack the Dutch East Indies to capture the oil fields of the island chain.

January 13 Atlantic Ocean
U-boats attack shipping off the U.S. East Coast in the "Happy Time."

January 16–19 Germany
Hitler sacks more than 30 senior generals who want to withdraw in the face of Soviet attacks on the Eastern Front.

January 20 Germany
The "FInal Solution," the extermination of Europe's Jews, becomes key to Nazi war plans at the Wannsee Conference in Berlin.

Chinese residents flee Nanking as the Japanese close in on the city in December 1937.

The Japanese government itself became dominated by militarists. In July 1941, they ordered the invasion of Indochina, whose colonial government had fallen after Germany's defeat of France in 1940. In response, the United States, Britain, and the Dutch East Indies prohibited all exports to Japan.

Toward War

Japan had to import 80 percent of its oil, which would soon run out. Its military planners decided to go to war to seize their own oil supplies. Their best chance lay in a rapid victory, which meant neutralizing the U.S. Navy.

The United States issued an ultimatum for Japan to withdraw from Indochina on November 26, 1941, but it had become irrelevant. On the same day, the Japanese fleet sailed from positions north of Japan bound for Pearl Harbor.

The Rape of Nanking

The Rape of Nanking took place during the Sino-Japanese War late in 1937. Japanese soldiers captured the old Chinese capital of Nanking (Nanjing) and began nearly two months of the rape, torture, and murder of civilians. The slaughter came to an end in February 1938. It was stopped as a result of international outrage—but also to prevent the spread of disease from the many corpses. Up to 200,000 Chinese were killed.

Japan's *Yamato* was one of the largest battleships in the world when it was built in 1937.

February

February 8 Singapore
Japanese troops land on the British-held island of Singapore.

February 11–12 North Sea
The Channel Dash sees German battle cruisers speed to the North Sea before the British can stop them.

February 14 Singapore
The British at Singapore surrender after the Japanese cut the island's water supply.

February 27–29 Java Sea
Japanese inflict heavy losses on an Allied fleet, sinking five cruisers and five destroyers to one Japanese cruiser lost.

Pearl Harbor

In U.S. history, December 7, 1941, is the "day of infamy" when Japan launched a surprise attack on the United States. The attack changed the course of World War II.

Smoke billows from the USS *West Virginia* at Pearl Harbor. The ship sank, but was salvaged.

TIMELINE **1942 MARCH–APRIL**

KEY:  **Pacific** | **Eastern Front** | **Europe and North Africa**

March

March 7 Burma
British soldiers evacuate the capital, Rangoon, as the Japanese enter.

March 9 Dutch East Indies
Allied resistance ends in surrender; the Japanese gain possession of their "Southern Resources Area."

March 11 Philippines
U.S. General Douglas MacArthur is evacuated from the Philippines to Australia; he makes his famous promise, "I shall return."

March 28–29 France
British commandos attack the dry dock at St. Nazaire; 144 men are killed and many more are captured.

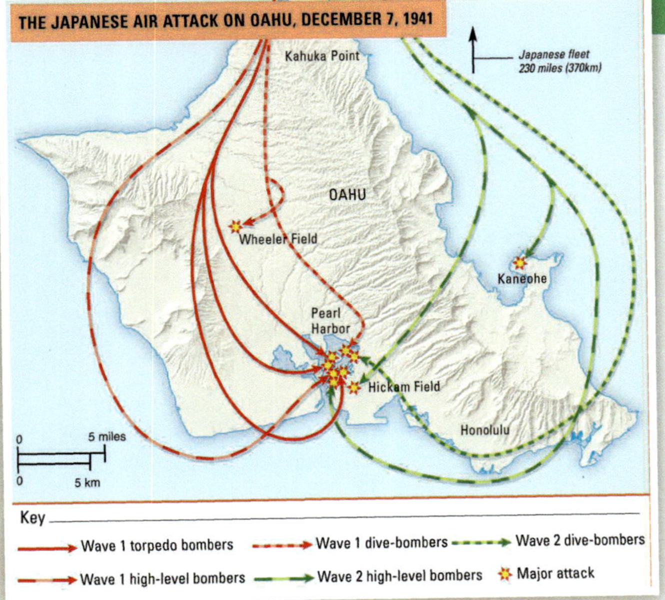

The Japanese attack targeted Oahu's airfields as well as the harbor.

As tension grew between the United States and Japan in May 1940, President Franklin D. Roosevelt ordered the Pacific Fleet to Pearl Harbor, in Hawaii. It became the largest U.S. naval base in the Pacific.

The Operation Begins

The Japanese planned an attack on Hawaii that would destroy the U.S. Pacific Fleet. Six aircraft carriers and two battleships sailed from the Japanese Kurile Islands for the Central Pacific on November 26, 1940.

KEY DATES

May 1940 Roosevelt sends the U.S. Pacific Fleet to Pearl Harbor, Hawaii.

August 1, 1941 The United States and its allies impose an embargo on oil exports to Japan.

November 30, 1941 U.S. intelligence decrypts Japanese messages anticipating an attack in the Pacific.

December 6, 1941 Roosevelt makes a final appeal for peace to Emperor Hirohito, but Japan's aircraft carriers are already steaming toward Hawaii.

December 7, 1941 Japanese aircraft attack Pearl Harbor and airfields on Oahu.

December 8, 1941 United States declares war on Japan.

December 11, 1941 Japan's allies, Germany and Italy, declare war on the United States.

April

April 9 Philippines
U.S. and Filipino forces in the Philippines surrender to the Japanese. Some 78,000 prisoners are forced to march 65 miles (105 km) into captivity; many die along the way.

April 18 Japan
In a raid led by James Doolittle, 16 U.S. B-25 bombers launched from an aircraft carrier attack Tokyo and other Japanese cities; Japan's leaders decide to destroy U.S. naval power in the Pacific.

Isoroku Yamamoto (1884–1943)

Admiral Yamamoto, who planned the Pearl Harbor attack, was one of Japan's leading naval strategists. He believed that the attack would buy Japan time against an enemy that was industrially superior. He also planned the Battle of Midway, where Japan lost its naval supremacy. He died when his aircraft was shot down over the South Pacific.

↑ A photo taken by a Japanese pilot shows the easy target the U.S. warships offered.

Keeping strict radio silence in order to avoid detection, the Japanese force reached a position 230 miles (370 km) north of Pearl Harbor.

→ Yamamoto was wary of going to war against an industrial superpower.

An Easy Target

U.S. Army intelligence was aware that a U.S. base in Asia might be attacked—but not where. Warnings only reached Hawaii after the attack. The U.S. forces at Pearl Harbor were therefore completely unready. They had even grouped their ships and aircraft together to make them easier to guard. This made them a sitting target for Japanese pilots.

TIMELINE **1942 MAY–JUNE**

KEY: Pacific | Eastern Front | Europe and North Africa

May

May 8 Pacific Ocean
The U.S. Navy loses a carrier in the Battle of the Coral Sea; the Japanese lose a smaller carrier, but a large number of aircraft.

May 26–31 North Africa
Rommel attacks the British Eighth Army in the Battle of Gazala.

May 31 Germany
Britain launches its first "1,000 bomber raid" on Cologne, where 59,000 people are left homeless.

The Aerial Attack

At 7:48 a.m. on Sunday, December 7, 1941, the first of three waves of Japanese airplanes began attacking Pearl Harbor and nearby airfields. Soldiers, sailors, and marines reacted bravely but ineffectively. When the attackers departed at 10:00 a.m., they left behind more than 2,400 people dead, 188 U.S. aircraft destroyed on the ground, and 16 ships sunk or damaged, including four sunken battleships.

The United States Declares War

Next day, December 8, Roosevelt addressed the U.S. Congress and asked for a declaration of war against Japan. The Senate voted unanimously to declare war; in the House of Representatives, only Jeannette Rankin of Montana voted against the coming conflict.

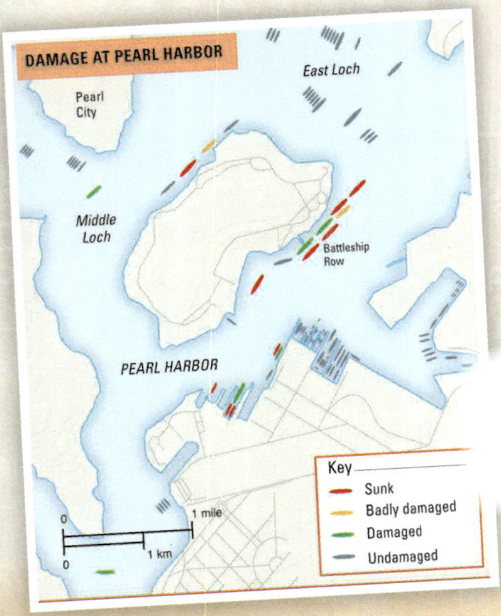

This diagram of Pearl Harbor shows the positions of the U.S. vessels sunk or damaged.

What Did Roosevelt Know?

Lasting controversy still surrounds how much Roosevelt knew about an attack on Pearl Harbor. Some historians think he ignored intelligence warnings because he wanted an excuse to take the United States into war. While there were rumors of a Japanese attack, however, it is likely that the president did not expect it to be on the U.S. Pacific Fleet. U.S. planners thought British or Dutch colonies in East and Southeast Asia were more obvious targets for a Japanese attack.

June

June 4 Pacific Ocean
The Battle of Midway. Japan's fleet aims to seize the U.S. base at Midway Island and destroy the U.S. Pacific Fleet. Despite having fewer ships, U.S. forces are victorious, sinking four Japanese carriers and destroying 332 aircraft.

June 10–13 North Africa
Rommel's way to Tobruk is open as British withdraw after the Battle of Gazala.

June 21 North Africa
Erwin Rommel captures Tobruk.

June 28 Soviet Union
The Germans launch summer offensive Operation Blue into southern Russia to capture oil fields in the Caucasus.

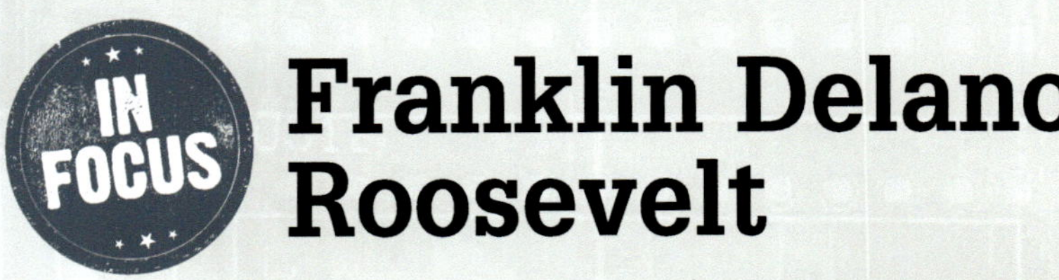

Franklin Delano Roosevelt

Roosevelt was a towering figure. He overcame economic depression at home and was the victor of World War II.

FDR, as he was commonly known, had been elected president in 1932, when the United States was in the depths of an economic depression. He injected energy and government money into helping the unemployed and kick-started a business revival. A trademark of FDR's terms of office was the way he gave radio broadcasts to let ordinary American citizens know his thoughts and why he was following certain policies. Up to his tenure of office, no president had served for more than two terms, but in 1940, with war raging in Europe and the Japanese army occupying large areas of China, he made the momentous decision to stand for a third term.

Going to War

Via the Lend-Lease Act of March 1941, FDR gave aid to Britain, which was struggling against the power of Nazi Germany. He also decided to take a firm stand against Japanese expansion into Asia. There was a strong isolationist strand in U.S. public life, and FDR had to be careful about the policies he followed. The fact that Japan made a surprise attack on the U.S. fleet at Pearl Harbor in December 1941, and that Nazi Germany then declared war on the United States, meant that FDR did not have to persuade the American people to go to war.

FDR was an inspiring war leader. He left military and naval operational matters to the professionals. Within a year of the United States entering the war the tide turned in favor of the Allies. President Roosevelt won a fourth term in office in 1944, but by then he was very ill. His legs had been paralyzed after an illness in 1921, and his health deteriorated during the 1940s. He died in April 1945 and was succeeded by his vice president, Harry S. Truman.

KEY DATES

January 30, 1882 Franklin Delano Roosevelt is born to a wealthy family in New York.

November, 1932 In an election dominated by the Great Depression, Roosevelt is elected president, beating Herbert Hoover and taking all but six states.

November, 1940 Roosevelt wins a unique third term as president as World War II rages in Europe.

March 11, 1941 Roosevelt secures congressional support for lend-lease (military aid) to Great Britain. This program is later extended to the Soviet Union.

December 7, 1941 Japanese attack on Pearl Harbor. Roosevelt calls it "a date which will live in infamy."

January, 1943 At the Casablanca Conference, Roosevelt announces that the aim of the Allies is the unconditional surrender of Nazi Germany, Italy, and Japan.

April 12, 1945 Franklin Roosevelt dies in Warm Springs, Georgia.

1 Franklin D. Roosevelt meets the UK's prime minister, Winston Churchill, in 1941. Roosevelt gave aid to beleaguered Britain.

2 The key moment of World War II was America's entry into the conflict. Here, Roosevelt signs the declaration of war against Japan, which had just attacked Pearl Harbor.

3 Roosevelt (flanked by Churchill and Joseph Stalin) at the Yalta Conference in 1945. The president is clearly a sick man.

Japan's Asian Advance

Pearl Harbor was just the start of Japan's campaign of conquest in the Pacific. A rapid onslaught against Allied forces secured territory across the region.

Japanese troops on a railroad locomotive celebrate their conquest of Malaya.

TIMELINE **1942 JULY–SEPTEMBER**

KEY: Pacific | Eastern Front | Europe and North Africa

July

July 4–10 Soviet Union
After a two-month siege, the Germans capture the port of Sevastopol and about 90,000 Red Army troops.

August

August 7 Guadalcanal
U.S. Marines land on Guadalcanal and face fierce Japanese resistance as they attempt to capture the airstrip at Henderson Field.

August 9 Pacific Ocean
In a heavy defeat for the U.S. Navy, the Japanese sink four U.S. cruisers at the Battle of Savo Island.

The Japanese used bicycles to advance rapidly on jungle roads.

Many Japanese officers knew there were risks in a long war against the United States and Britain. They aimed to capture strategic territories that were rich in resources as fast as possible.

The First Defeats

On December 8 (the same day as Pearl Harbor, but on the other side of the international date line), Japan invaded Thailand

KEY DATES

December 9, 1941 Thailand surrenders to Japan.

December 23, 1941 The Japanese capture Wake Island.

December 25, 1941 The British surrender Hong Kong.

January 11, 1942 The Japanese capture the Malayan capital of Kuala Lumpur.

February 14, 1942 The British surrender Singapore: it is the British Army's biggest single defeat so far.

March 8, 1942 The last of the islands of the Dutch East Indies surrenders.

May 26, 1942 The last Allied forces leave Burma.

A British infantryman surrenders during the Japanese advance in Malaya.

August 19 France
A combined Canadian, British, and U.S. force attacks the port of Dieppe. It is a disaster, with many of those landed killed.

August 23 Soviet Union
A raid by 600 German bombers on Stalingrad kills thousands.

September

September 2 Poland
The Nazis "clear" the Jewish Warsaw Ghetto; more than 50,000 Jews are killed.

Bushido: The Way of the Warrior

Bushido was the code of behavior followed by Japan's samurai warriors. It involved complete obedience to superiors, contempt for death and pain, and a mastery of military skills. Recruits were taught that death was preferable to surrender. That belief cost the Allies and Japanese heavy casualties during the Pacific War. It also underlay Japan's use of suicide tactics (kamikaze) toward the end of the war. A side effect of Bushido was cruelty toward POWs and civilian populations.

and northern Malaya. It also attacked the island of Hong Kong. By Christmas Day, the Japanese had captured the British colony.

In Malaya, Japanese troops rapidly progressed down through the mainland. Its capital, Kuala Lumpur, fell on January 11, 1942. By then, Japan had conquered two-thirds of the country. Allied forces in Malaya retreated to Singapore, off the tip of the Malay Peninsula. The island was a key British colony, which controlled vital sea routes. Although British defenders outnumbered the attackers, they surrendered on February 12, after the Japanese captured the island's reservoirs.

Dutch East Indies

The naval Battle of the Java Sea on February 27, 1942, was a decisive victory for

➔ The British surrender at Singapore three days after the Japanese cut off the water supply.

TIMELINE 1942 OCTOBER–DECEMBER

KEY: Pacific | Eastern Front | Europe and North Africa

October

October 23 North Africa
The Second Battle of El Alamein begins in Egypt.

November

November 2–4 North Africa
The Second Battle of El Alamein. Rommel is forced to retreat; it is a decisive defeat for the German forces in North Africa. They will not recover.

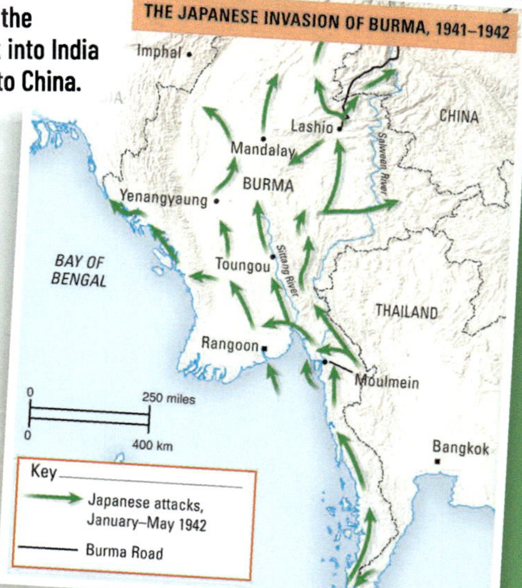

The Japanese drove the British from Burma back into India and the Chinese back into China.

the Japanese. It effectively ended Allied resistance in the Dutch East Indies (now Indonesia). By March 8, all the islands of the group had surrendered.

Burma Falls

Meanwhile, the Japanese invaded Burma in January 1942. Hampered by poor British decision making, Allied forces were forced to retreat toward the Indian border. By May, the Japanese were in charge of the whole country. In just six months, the Japanese had achieved victories throughout Southeast Asia. The Dutch and British colonial empires were gone.

Jungle Warfare

The Japanese were masters of fighting in the dense, hot, and humid forests of Southeast Asia. Normal tactical maneuvers were impossible and heat exhaustion was common. The most serious problems were diseases such as malaria. Fungus and bacteria thrived; the smallest cut could become infected.

Indian troops in the British Army advance through a Malay plantation.

November 19 Soviet Union
General Georgi Zhukov launches an attack to relieve Stalingrad; the pincer movement traps the Germans in the city as the German fronts collapse west of the city.

December

December 19 Soviet Union
A German counterattack fails to rescue the Sixth Army trapped in Stalingrad, where conditions are deteriorating and food is short.

Fall of the Philippines

The capture of the Philippines was a crucial part of Japan's strategy to secure an empire in the Southwest Pacific and to remove U.S. power from the region.

U.S. prisoners await their fate after being captured at Bataan.

TIMELINE 1943 JANUARY–MARCH

KEY: Pacific | Eastern Front | Europe and North Africa

January

January 10 Guadalcanal
Some 50,000 U.S. troops attack the Japanese defenders, who are starving; many are also sick.

January 18 Poland
Jewish fighters in the Warsaw Ghetto begin attacking German troops.

January 31 Guadalcanal
U.S. troops finally capture the island of Guadalcanal.

February

February 2 Soviet Union
The Siege of Stalingrad ends when 93,000 German troops surrender.

February 14–22 North Africa
Inexperienced U.S. troops suffer heavy losses in the Battle of Kasserine Pass.

The Philippines—a group of some 7,000 islands—were of vital strategic importance. They had been a U.S. colony since 1898. The U.S. government planned to return them to Filipino rule, but growing Japanese power had isolated the islands. By mid-1941, the Philippines were threatened on three sides.

U.S. Response

As diplomatic relations with Japan deteriorated, the United States reinforced the Philippines. In July 1941, General MacArthur was made head of a new command in the region, the U.S. Army Forces in the Far East (USAFFE). MacArthur urged his superiors to adopt an ambitious program to build up the Philippines as a base of U.S. power. With limited naval resources available, he asked for the creation of a huge air force in the islands.

KEY DATES

July 1941 General Douglas MacArthur takes over USAFFE.

December 10, 1941 Japanese troops land on Luzon, followed by more two days later.

December 19, 1941 Japanese troops land on Mindanao.

January 2, 1942 Japanese enter Manila, the capital.

January 9, 1942 Japanese attack U.S. positions on the Bataan Peninsula.

January 22, 1942 U.S. troops fall back.

March 12, 1942 MacArthur leaves for Australia.

April 10, 1942 The Bataan Death March begins.

May 6, 1942 Japanese troops land on Corregidor.

May 8, 1942 U.S. forces surrender.

← Japanese troops land on the U.S.-held island of Corregidor on May 6, 1942.

February 16 Germany
Students demonstrate against Hitler's regime in Munich; the leaders are executed.

February 18 Burma
A 3,000-strong force of British Chindits parachute behind Japanese lines for a six-week mission to cut the enemy supply lines.

March

March 2–5 Bismarck Sea
In the Battle of the Bismarck Sea, Allied warships sink eight Japanese transports and four destroyers.

March 14 Soviet Union
German forces destroy the Soviet Third Tank Army, forcing Soviets to abandon newly won territory on the Eastern Front.

March 15 Soviet Union
The Germans plan Operation Citadel, an offensive to destroy Red Army troops near the city of Kursk.

Bataan Death March

The Japanese forced more than 72,000 American and Filipino prisoners to march with no food or water more than 65 miles (105 km) toward a prison camp. Weak, sick, and tired, any prisoners who dropped out were killed. Some 18,000 men died. General Homma, who ordered the march, was executed after the war.

Japan Attacks

By December 1941, MacArthur's army and air force had grown. They were to prove ineffectual, however. When Japanese air raids began, more than half the U.S. aircraft were destroyed in two days. The main Japanese landing followed on December 22; Japanese forces entered the capital, Manila, on January 2, 1942. On January 5, U.S. and Filipino forces completed their withdrawal to Bataan, a mountainous peninsula covered in jungle on the island of Luzon. In their rapid withdrawal, the troops left most of their equipment. Troops were on half rations; within weeks, they were eating mules.

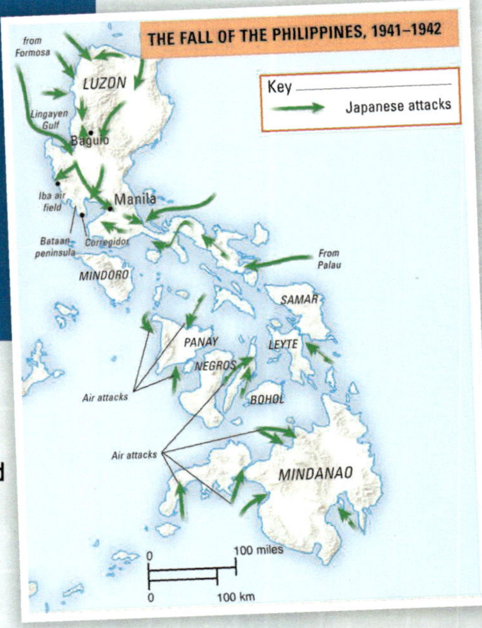

 U.S. defense was concentrated around Manila Bay on the island of Luzon.

Campaign for Bataan

Japanese forces were weakened after their advance. Their commander, General Homma, launched his first attack on Bataan on January 9.

TIMELINE 1943 APRIL–JUNE

KEY: Pacific | Eastern Front | Europe and North Africa

April

April 12 Soviet Union
The Germans find a mass grave in Katyn Forest containing 10,000 Polish army officers executed by Soviet secret police in 1939.

April 17 Germany
U.S. bombers attack the German city of Bremen.

May

May 13 North Africa
Axis forces surrender to the Allies; 620,000 Axis casualties and prisoners have been lost in the campaign.

MacArthur remained confident that his troops could hold out. However, by the end of February the Bataan defenders were suffering from serious malnutrition, malaria, and dysentery. The U.S. government, wanting a sign of U.S. strength, forbade the troops to surrender but forced MacArthur to evacuate to Australia.

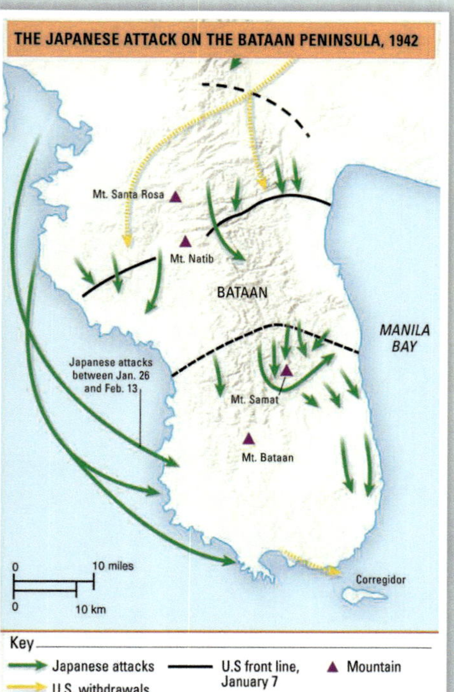

Meanwhile, Homma launched a fresh attack on April 3. Exhausted, the defenders finally broke. U.S. troops under Commander Wainwright withdrew to the island of Corregidor to organize what few defenses remained in the Philippines. The forces left on Luzon surrendered on April 9.

For a month, the underground fortress on Corregidor was the site of the final U.S. stand (see box, above right). It fell on May 8, 1942.

Corregidor

As the Japanese advanced in May 1942, U.S. forces fell back to the tiny fortified island of Corregidor 2 miles (3.2 km) east of the Bataan Peninsula. More than 11,000 men took shelter in its tunnels, but water and supplies began to run out. Facing a Japanese onslaught, the U.S. garrison finally surrendered. On May 8, U.S. commander General Jonathan Wainwright ordered all remaining U.S. and Filipino troops on the islands to surrender.

← Corregidor was the only escape from the mountainous, jungle-covered Bataan Peninsula.

May 16-17 Germany
The Dambusters Raid. The British use "bouncing bombs" to destroy dams in Germany's industrial Ruhr region.

May 16 Poland
The Warsaw Ghetto uprising ends. The German forces were utterly ruthless in suppressing the Jewish resistance.

June

June 10 Germany
British and U.S. bombers begin Operation Pointblank, a year-long series of attacks on German industry.

Douglas MacArthur

MacArthur served in both World Wars, and commanded Allied forces in the South Pacific.

MacArthur served with distinction in the U.S. Army on the Western Front in World War I (1914–1918). He became Chief of Staff of the army in 1930. In 1935, he was appointed advisor to the government of the Philippines. He was brought back into active U.S. service in July 1941, being named Commander of the U.S. Army Forces in the Far East. The troops he commanded in the Philippines were swept away by the Japanese invasion of December 1941, and MacArthur retreated to the Bataan Peninsula. His troops finally surrendered in May 1942. MacArthur himself had been ordered to Australia in March, and he made a famous promise to the Philippines: "I will return."

1

Returning Hero

In April 1942 MacArthur was named Supreme Commander of Allied Forces in the Southwest Pacific. His forces stopped the Japanese advancing through New Guinea toward Australia. He then took the offensive, advancing along the coast of New Guinea. MacArthur was a popular figure, and some suggested he should run for president in 1944. However, he was closely involved in the preparations for U.S. forces returning to the Philippines and in October 1944 he waded ashore to fulfil the promise he had made in 1942. The fighting in the Philippines was fierce, but the Japanese surrendered in September 1945.

After the war, Douglas MacArthur commanded the U.S. forces that occupied Japan. During that time he pushed through various reforms that transformed Japanese society.

2

KEY DATES

January 26, 1880 Douglas MacArthur is born in Little Rock, Arkansas.

1918 Bravery and effective leadership during World War I earn MacArthur seven Silver Stars and the Distinguished Service Cross.

1935 MacArthur becomes Field Marshal in the Philippines Army.

March 12, 1942 After the Japanese invasion of the Philippines, MacArthur leaves for Australia. He vows: "I will return," and will do so in 1944.

March, 1943 MacArthur presents his strategy for the Pacific War: taking only major Japanese bases, and bypassing minor ones.

September 2, 1945 MacArthur signs the instrument of surrender of Japan on board USS *Missouri* in Tokyo Bay.

April 5, 1964 Douglas MacArthur dies in Washington, D.C.

1 MacArthur with the corncob pipe that he used as a prop in many photo-calls. He was skilled at courting publicity.

2 MacArthur (far left) at a meeting with President Roosevelt (in the white shirt), deciding on the deployment of resources to attack Japan.

3 MacArthur while he was serving as an officer in France in 1918.

4 General Pershing awards the Distinguished Service Cross to Douglas MacArthur for his heroism during World War I.

The Battle of the Coral Sea

By the spring of 1942, the rapid advances in Southeast Asia and the Pacific created a split in priorities and almost brought the Japanese to defeat in the Coral Sea.

↑ A U.S. Avenger bomber launches its torpedo during maneuvers.

TIMELINE 1943 JULY–SEPTEMBER

KEY:  Pacific | Eastern Front | Europe and North Africa

July

July 5 Soviet Union
The Battle of Kursk is the largest tank battle in history; the Germans make little progress against the Soviets.

July 10 Sicily
Operation Husky: U.S. and British troops invade the island.

July 12–13 Soviet Union
The Soviets narrowly defeat the Germans at Kursk. The battle leaves 500,000 casualties dead, injured, or missing.

July 25 Italy
The king of Italy sacks Benito Mussolini. The new leader, Pietro Badoglio, hopes the Allies will occupy Italy before it falls under German control.

August

July 24–August 2 Germany
The British bomb Hamburg, killing around 50,000 civilians and leaving 800,000 homeless.

Since the attack on Pearl Harbor, the Japanese had enjoyed a string of victories. After their rapid successes, however, the Japanese were not sure what to do next.

They had planned Operation MO, an attack on Guadalcanal in the Solomon Islands, which threatened Allied convoy routes to Australia and New Zealand. Before the operation was fully put into action, however, a daring U.S. attack changed Japanese intentions. The Doolittle raid was a reminder of the potential threat from aircraft based on U.S. carriers. The Japanese decided to split their forces and continue with Operation MO while at the same time thrusting into the Central Pacific.

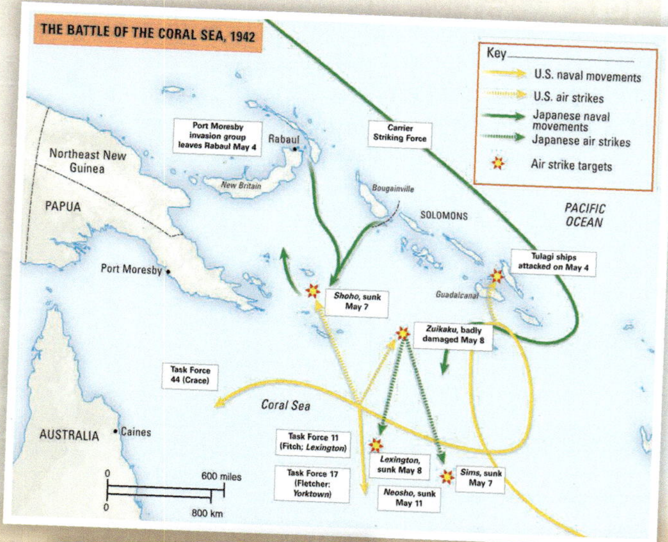

KEY DATES

April 18, 1942 The Doolittle raid; U.S. bombers from the carrier *Hornet* attack Tokyo and other cities.

May 1, 1942 U.S. carriers *Yorktown* and *Lexington* meet up in Coral Sea.

May 3, 1942 Japanese landings on Tulagi confirm U.S. intelligence to be correct.

May 4, 1942 U.S.-Australian Task Force 44 joins U.S. carriers in Coral Sea. *Yorktown* launches strikes against the Tulagi invasion force.

May 7, 1942 Battle of the Coral Sea begins; Japanese sink the U.S. destroyer *Sims*; the Japanese lose a light carrier.

May 8, 1942 Japanese *Zuikaku* loses almost all its aircraft; the *Shokaku* is hit three times. The *Yorktown* is hit and the *Lexington* sunk; the battle ends with no clear victor.

← The surface vessels engaged in the Coral Sea never came in sight of one another.

August 17 Sicily
The capture of Messina marks Allied victory on Sicily; from there, the Allies can attack the Italian peninsula.

August 22-23 Soviet Union
The Red Army recaptures Kharkov and threatens German positions in Ukraine.

September

September 9 Italy
U.S. and British troops land in southern Italy.

September 12 Italy
German airborne troops led by Lieutenant Colonel Otto Skorzeny rescue Mussolini from imprisonment in a hotel in the Italian mountains.

September 25 Soviet Union
The Red Army recaptures the city of Smolensk.

The Doolittle Raid

U.S. strategists planned a carrier-based bomber raid on Japan itself. The raid, on April 18, 1942, was nicknamed Doolittle after its commander. Sixteen B-25 bombers were fitted with extra fuel tanks to increase their range. They bombed Tokyo before heading for China. The raid did little damage, but gave a major boost to U.S. morale. It also scared Japan's leaders into seeking a decisive battle with the U.S. fleet—a battle they would lose.

→ One of the 16 B-25s leaves the carrier USS *Hornet* for Tokyo.

By mid-April 1942, U.S. intelligence was suggesting that the Japanese would try to attack Port Moresby on New Guinea from their base at Rabaul on New Britain Island.

Battle of the Coral Sea

U.S. admiral Chester Nimitz sent two aircraft carriers and their task forces to the Coral Sea to prevent the attack. The U.S. carriers engaged a Japanese carrier force on May 7 in the first-ever naval battle in which the opposing fleets did not come into visual contact. The carriers launched all their aircraft, but neither found the enemy's main

→ A destroyer waits as the crew of the stricken *Lexington* abandon ship.

TIMELINE 1943 OCTOBER–DECEMBER

KEY: Pacific | Eastern Front | Europe and North Africa

October

October 12-22 Italy
Allied forces advance slowly north in bad weather toward German positions on the Gustav Line, in central Italy.

October 25 Burma
The Burma to Siam (Thailand) rail link is completed. It has been built by Allied prisoners of the Japanese and local people; about 12,000 prisoners have died from abuse, disease, and starvation.

November

November 6 Soviet Union
The Soviets capture Kiev, trapping the German Seventeenth Army in the Crimea.

force. The sinking of the Japanese light carrier *Shoho* on the first day was the first Allied naval success of the Pacific war. On May 8, Japanese aircraft sank the USS *Lexington*. Japanese commanders believed their pilots had sunk both U.S. carriers. However, a lack of air cover forced the Japanese to turn the invasion fleet back from Port Moresby and abandon their planned landings.

Who Won the Battle?

The Battle of the Coral Sea was small, but it shaped future naval strategy. In the confusion, both sides claimed victory. The Japanese had lost a small carrier while destroying a large U.S. carrier. The Americans had stopped the landings at Port Moresby, thereby ending Operation MO and protecting Australia. Most military historians judge the action a draw, but in spring 1942, U.S. fortunes were so low that the result seemed like a major victory.

The important consequences lay in the long-term damage that had been done to the Imperial Japanese Navy and the loss of valuable aircraft and fighter pilots.

Cracking Japan's Codes

The ultimate Allied victory in World War II owed much to code breaking. By April 1942, U.S. analysts had partially cracked the Japanese naval code, JN-25. The intelligence they learned gave them a decisive advantage. At the Battle of Midway in June 1942, for example, U.S. carriers were waiting for the Japanese fleet. In April 1943, more intercepted signals allowed fighters to shoot down the plane of the Japanese naval chief, Yamamoto, who was killed.

Students at a U.S. Aeronautical Radio School take a class in deciphering Japanese codes.

November 20 Gilbert Islands
Some 18,600 U.S. Marines land on Tawara and Bieto in the Gilbert Islands in the Pacific Ocean; more than 1,000 Marines die before the islands are captured on the 23rd.

December 26 Arctic Ocean
The Battle of the North Cape sees British warships sink the German battleship *Scharnhorst*.

December

November 28 Iran
British Prime Minister Winston Churchill meets President Roosevelt and Soviet leader Joseph Stalin in Tehran; they give priority to a cross-Channel invasion of occupied Europe in May 1944.

Carrier Aircraft

Very soon during the Pacific War, carrier aircraft became the key naval weapons.

Up until the outbreak of World War II, the strength of a navy was usually estimated in terms of its battleships. As the war developed, however, it was clear that battleships were more vulnerable to attack from the air than from naval gunfire. Aircraft carriers able to send waves of airplanes carrying torpedoes and bombs became the new capital ships. Pearl Harbor was a prime example of deadly sorties by carrier-borne aircraft that sank battleships. It was fortunate for the U.S. Navy that three aircraft carriers were not at Pearl Harbor. They survived to take on the Japanese Navy in 1942.

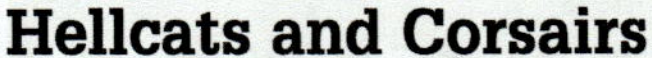

Hellcats and Corsairs

The most effective carrier aircraft in the early years of the Pacific War was the Japanese Mitsubishi A6M Zero. It was maneuverable and had a long range. Although Allied pilots tried various new tactics against Zeros, they recognized that it was a better airplane, superior to the F4 Wildcat, which was the standard U.S. carrier-borne fighter in 1942.

In 1943, the U.S. Navy began flying the F6 Hellcat and in 1944 the F4U Corsair went into service. These aircraft were much more heavily armed than the Zero and they dominated the skies in the naval battles of the last two years of the war. The Hellcat alone was estimated to have shot down over 5,000 Japanese aircraft.

1

2

KEY DATES

May, 1912 The first aircraft is flown from the flight deck of a warship at sea.

1921 Japan launches *Hosho*, the first purpose-built aircraft carrier.

1940 The first Zero fighters (A6M2) are put into active service. They shoot down Soviet-made fighters over China.

May/June 1942 The Battles of the Coral Sea and Midway. U.S. and Japanese fleets engage without the surface warships seeing each other. The U.S. loses 220 aircraft in these battles; Japanese losses are about 320 aircraft.

Autumn, 1942 During the fighting on Guadalcanal, pilots of F4 Wildcats develop new dive tactics against Zeros because they cannot match them in conventional dogfights.

June 19-20, 1944 Battle of the Philippine Sea. U.S. aircraft cripple Japanese naval aviation. U.S. losses are 123 aircraft; Japan loses over 600 and has few trained pilots left.

1 A Corsair fires a volley of rockets during ground support operations at the Battle of Okinawa in 1945.

2 A downed Zero fighter on the island of Munda in 1943. At this stage, the Hellcat was the only U.S. fighter able to match the Zero.

3 Japanese Zero A6M3 Model 22 fighters in formation. The Zero could extend its flight time to over six hours, if necessary.

4 Newly commissioned F6 Hellcat fighters fly into action in May 1943. Together with the F4U Corsair, the Hellcat dominates the skies over the Pacific.

The Battle of Midway

Japan's thrust into the Central Pacific aimed to destroy the remaining U.S. fleet. Instead, it was a disaster for the Imperial Japanese Navy.

The Japanese heavy cruiser *Mikuma* sinks after being damaged by U.S. bombers.

TIMELINE **1944 JANUARY–FEBRUARY**

KEY:  **Pacific** **Eastern Front** **Europe and North Africa**

January

January 14–17 Soviet Union
Red Army attacks on the Germans besieging Leningrad force the Germans to retreat. Some 830,000 civilians have died in the three-year siege.

January 22 Italy
Allied troops land at Anzio, behind the Gustav Line, and meet little resistance; U.S. General John Lucas orders his forces to create defensive positions.

January 30 Marshall Islands
Americans begin an attack on the Marshall Islands in the Pacific by landing on the undefended Majuro Atoll.

After Japan's thrust to isolate Australia was halted at the Battle of the Coral Sea, Japan's naval planners focused on defeating U.S. carrier forces. They would occupy the Aleutian Islands off Alaska and seize Midway Island, an Allied airbase in the Central Pacific, to draw the U.S. carriers into an unequal battle.

The Japanese fleet had more operational aircraft carriers and more experienced pilots flying superior Zero fighters. However, unknown to Japanese commander Isoroku Yamamoto, U.S. intelligence had cracked Japanese navy codes. U.S. commanders therefore knew what Yamamoto was planning.

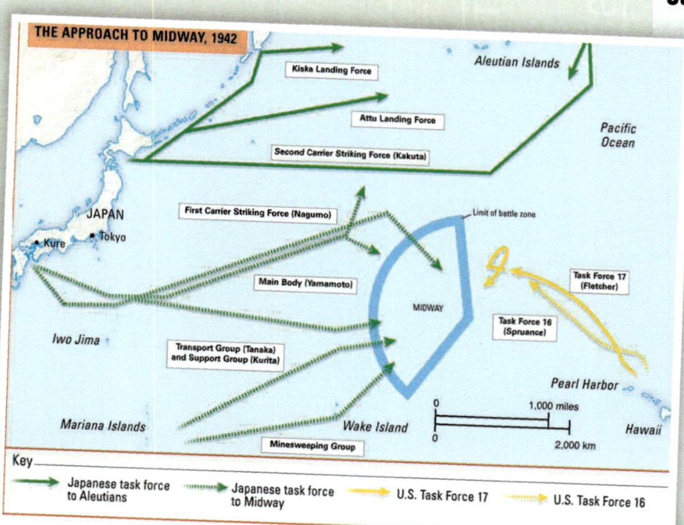

KEY DATES

May 1942 The largest Japanese fleet ever assembled sails for the Central Pacific.

June 3, 1942 Japanese Northern Area Force occupies Kiska and Attu in the Aleutian Islands, but the Americans ignore the decoy. U.S. bombers attack Japanese fleet at Midway, but cause little damage.

June 4, 1942 Japanese bombers score early successes at Midway.

June 4, 1942, 10:28 a.m. Bombers from USS *Enterprise* disable two Japanese carriers; the successes change the course of the war in the Pacific.

June 6, 1942 Americans sink a Japanese heavy cruiser.

June 7, 1942 *Yorktown* is sunk by a Japanese submarine in the last engagement of the Battle of Midway.

← Japan made thrusts to the Aleutian Islands and into the Central Pacific.

February

February 1–4 Marshall Islands
Some 40,000 U.S. troops launch an amphibious assault against Kwajalein Atoll; they lose 1,000 men, against more than 11,600 Japanese dead.

February 4–24 Burma
The Japanese launch Operation Ha-Go to drive the Allies back to the border with India.

February 18–22 Marshall Islands
U.S. forces seize Eniwetok Atoll, completing the conquest of the islands.

The Japanese Plan

In spring 1942, Isoroku Yamamoto sought to press home Japan's advantage in the Pacific. He gathered four large naval task forces. Three headed into the Central Pacific. The other struck north for the Aleutian Islands, off Alaska, to draw off U.S. forces. An amphibious force would attack Midway. The island was beyond U.S. air cover, so the Americans would send their fleet to protect it. Yamamoto planned to combine his fleets into an overwhelming force and destroy the U.S. Navy.

The United States got their carriers in place before the Japanese arrived, giving them the advantage of surprise. In addition, the Japanese thought they faced only two enemy aircraft carriers: in fact, they faced three, as *Yorktown* had survived the Battle of the Coral Sea and been repaired in only three days.

Nagumo's Error

On June 3, the Japanese seized remote islands in the Aleutians. However, the Americans stayed close to Midway when a Japanese landing fleet was spotted. Next day, Japanese aircraft gained an advantage in early clashes. Fleet commander Chuichi Nagumo ordered a new wave of air strikes. He believed he had driven off the U.S. defenders—but he was mistaken. U.S. dive bombers surprised the Japanese fleet at 10:28 a.m. They destroyed

→ U.S. Devastator torpedo bombers are readied on the deck of the USS *Enterprise*.

TIMELINE 1944 MARCH–APRIL

KEY: Pacific | Eastern Front | Europe and North Africa

March

March 7-8 India/Burma
Operation U-Go begins; the Japanese assault aims to drive the Allies back into India by attacking their bases at Imphal and Kohima.

March 20-22 Italy
Allied attacks fail to overcome Monte Cassino, part of the Gustav Line.

March 24 Burma
Orde Wingate, CO of the Allied Chindits, dies in a plane crash.

March 29 India
Japanese forces cut the road between the British bases at Imphal and Kohima, and begin the siege of Kohima.

➔ A Japanese fighter falls from the sky after being hit by U.S. fire.

Akagi and *Kaga* and also hit *Soryu* and *Hiryu*, which later sank. A Japanese attack crippled the *Yorktown*, but that success had a high cost. The Japanese had lost four aircraft carriers, 332 aircraft, and hundreds of pilots.

The Battle of Midway turned the tide in the Pacific, which the Japanese had dominated for six months. Their failure left them with a seriously weakened naval aviation.

The Zero

The Mitsubishi A6M Zero-Sen was the first carrier fighter capable of surpassing land-based aircraft. The Zero was deadly in a dogfight and could outmaneuver enemy fighters. With a top speed of 350 mph (560 km/h), the Zero was the basis of Japanese carrier aviation in the Battle of the Coral Sea and at Midway. More Zeros were made than any other wartime Japanese aircraft: 10,938 in total.

🡐 The Japanese flag flies on U.S. sovereign territory in the Aleutians.

April

April 4–13 India
British forces attack the Japanese and begin to drive them back from Imphal and Kohima.

April 6–11 Burma
Japanese attacks force the Chindits to evacuate their fortified position at "White City."

April 22 New Guinea
An Allied invasion force commanded by U.S. General Douglas MacArthur lands in Hollandia as part of Operation Cartwheel, aiming to drive the Japanese from New Guinea.

Guadalcanal and the Solomons

In pitiless jungle conditions and deadly naval night actions, U.S. forces won the Battle for Guadalcanal.

In summer 1942, the Allies decided to take the offensive in the Pacific and landed U.S. Marines on the island of Guadalcanal in the Solomons chain in August 1942.

The Marines took over an air base built by the Japanese (the Marines called it Henderson Field for a Marine airman who had died in the Battle of Midway) and the fighting on the island focused on control of this airstrip. There were three major land encounters between Japanese and U.S. troops. Both sides suffered from diseases such as dysentery, while fighting at night caused heavy losses.

The Tokyo Express

The Japanese navy had to supply and reinforce their troops on the island and also tried to bombard Henderson Field. They sent transports and destroyers to Guadalcanal at night. This Tokyo Express, as the Allies called these sorties, resulted in a series of battles. The Japanese had success in many encounters, partly because their torpedoes were superior to the U.S. weapons, but in the end the U.S. Navy stopped the resupply effort. In February 1943 the Japanese evacuated over 10,000 troops. They had, however, suffered over 25,000 casualties. Allied casualties were over 14,000.

1

2

3

4

5

6

KEY DATES

May, 1942 Japanese forces take Guadalcanal. They begin constructing an airfield to cut communications between the USA and Australia.

August 7, 1942 Marines of the 1st Marine Division under Major General Alexander Vandegrift land on Guadalcanal and soon after on the nearby islands of Tulagi and Florida.

August 8-9, 1942 Naval Battle of Savo Island. Allied aircraft carriers withdraw from the waters off Guadalcanal.

August 20, 1942 Allied aircraft begin to operate from Henderson Field.

August 21, 1942 Battle of Tenaru. Ground attack by Japanese forces against the Marines on Guadalcanal.

September 12, 1942 Battle of Edson's Ridge. U.S. forces fight off Japanese ground attacks.

November 12-15, 1942 Decisive naval battle of Guadalcanal. Although suffering losses themselves, U.S. Navy vessels prevent Japanese reinforcements and supplies getting to Guadalcanal and stop Japanese battleships bombarding Henderson Field.

1 The USS *Wasp* burning after intense Japanese attacks during an encounter on September 15, 1942.

2 A U.S. patrol crosses a shallow river on Guadalcanal. The fighting in the jungle often took place at close range.

3 A detachment of U.S. Marines takes a well-earned break during an advance toward Japanese positions on Guadalcanal.

4 The carrier USS *Enterprise* under attack during the Battle of th Eastern Solomons, August 24, 1942.

5 A Japanese transport, the *Kinugawa Maru*, destroyed and beached on Guadalcanal in November 1942.

6 An aerial view of Henderson Field, the small airstrip around which much of the fighting on the island revolved.

Island Hopping

By the start of 1944, U.S. forces began an advance toward Japan. Their goal remained thousands of miles away, however, protected by the vast Pacific Ocean.

A U.S. B-25 bombs Japanese positions in the Marshall Islands.

TIMELINE 1944 MAY–JUNE

KEY: Pacific | Eastern Front | Europe and North Africa

May

May 9 Soviet Union
The Red Army liberates the Black Sea port of Sevastopol.

May 11–18 Italy
The Allies break through the Gustav Line near Monte Cassino.

May 18 Pacific Ocean
U.S. forces clear the Admiralty Islands of Japanese, effectively isolating the Japanese bases at Rabaul and Kavieng in the Southwest Pacific.

The strategic position in the Pacific in mid-1944.

By 1944, the United States was ready to make two simultaneous thrusts: one into the Central Pacific, the other into the Southwest Pacific. U.S. Navy admiral Chester Nimitz led the first, toward Japan itself, while U.S. Army general Douglas MacArthur led the second. His aim was to neutralize Rabaul, the key Japanese base on New Guinea.

KEY DATES

October 1943 U.S. air campaign begins against Rabaul, New Guinea.

November 1943 United States retakes Solomon Islands and Tarawa.

February 7, 1944 United States captures Marshall Islands.

June 19–21, 1944 Battle of the Philippine Sea; Japan loses its naval aviation arm.

July 13, 1944 U.S. forces capture Saipan, Marianas.

July 30, 1944 U.S. forces secure north coast of New Guinea.

August 2, 1944 Tinian is taken.

August 10, 1944 Guam is taken.

An Allied bomber attacks vessels in the harbor at Rabaul, one of many attacks on the port.

June

June 3 Italy
German troops abandon Rome, which is occupied by U.S. troops on June 5.

June 6 Northern France
The Allied invasion of Normandy, Operation Overlord, begins with paratroopers taking key targets and landings on five beaches. By the day's end, the Allies have a beachhead in Europe at the cost of 2,500 dead.

June 19–21 Philippine Sea
The "Great Marianas Turkey Shoot." The Japanese lose three aircraft carriers and 346 combat aircraft in the Battle of the Philippine Sea.

June 22 Soviet Union
With huge superiority of numbers, the Red Army launches Operation Bagration against German Army Group Center.

June 30 Britain
To date, 2,000 V1 "flying bombs" have been launched against British targets, mostly London.

Battle of Tarawa

Tarawa, fought between November 20 and 23, 1943, was the first U.S. offensive in the Central Pacific. It was also the first time a U.S. amphibious landing faced serious Japanese opposition. The U.S. attackers lost 1,500 out of 5,000 men on the first morning. Despite the chaos, the United States secured the island early on November 23. Fewer than one hundred of the island's 4,500 defenders surrendered. The losses shocked U.S. commanders and the public at home.

→ U.S. aircraft fly a raid against the Marianas in June 1940.

Central Pacific

Nimitz's advance aimed to use amphibious landings to capture islands. It would establish bases and airfields that would eventually bring U.S. forces within striking distance of Japan. Unlike MacArthur, whose landings often had the benefit of surprise, Nimitz' amphibious landings often took place under heavy fire. The small islands of the Central Pacific were far apart, so attackers could be easily spotted and surprise was harder to achieve.

Heavy Toll for Japan

The first thrust of Nimitz's advance secured the Marshall Islands. U.S. commanders then targeted the Marianas, where Marines landed on Saipan on June 15. It took a month of heavy fighting to win the island; some 29,000 Japanese soldiers and 22,000 civilians died. Marines went on to capture

TIMELINE **1944 JULY–AUGUST**

KEY: Pacific | Eastern Front | Europe and North Africa

July

July 7 Saipan
Japanese forces launch a mass charge that breaks U.S. lines before it fails.

July 9 Saipan
U.S. troops secure the island; at least 8,000 Japanese troops and civilians commit suicide rather than surrender.

July 20 Germany
Count Schenk von Stauffenberg plants a bomb in a conference room, but fails to kill Hitler. The failure leads to the execution of dozens of suspects.

July 21 Guam
U.S. troops begin landing on Guam, the largest of the Mariana Islands.

Tinian and Guam. Japan sent its Mobile Fleet to defend the islands. It met the U.S. Fifth Fleet in the Philippine Sea. The battle that followed ended in disaster for the Japanese, who lost 346 aircraft to just 30 U.S. planes. The Battle of the Philippine Sea was the largest carrier action of the Pacific War. It was so one-sided the U.S. pilots nicknamed it the "Great Marianas Turkey Shoot." Japan effectively lost its naval aviation arm in the battle.

The loss of the Marianas and the devastation of the Mobile Fleet were disastrous for Japan. The enemy had breached its ring of defensive islands and exposed Japan to attack.

U.S. Submarine Campaign

When the war in the Pacific began, the U.S. submarine fleet was small and largely obsolete. It expanded rapidly and was vital in cutting Japan's movement of supplies. New, more modern submarines were introduced like the well-armed Tench class with a range of some 11,000 nautical miles (20,370 km). In 1944, U.S. submarines sank over half of the 3.3 million tons of merchant shipping lost by Japan. By 1945, Japan's merchant fleet was finished—and Japan's supply routes destroyed.

U.S. troops evacuate Japanese civilians on Saipan. Many Japanese killed themselves rather than surrender.

August

August 1 Poland
The Warsaw Uprising —38,000 soldiers of the Polish Home Army fight the Germans.

August 10 Marianas Islands
Japanese resistance on Guam finally ends after fierce fighting; however, the last Japanese soldier on the island does not give himself up until 1960.

August 25 France
General Dietrich von Choltitz, commander of the German garrison in Paris, surrenders the city to the Allies.

The Battle for New Guinea

The campaigns in New Guinea stretched the resources of both the Japanese and Allied forces.

The fighting in New Guinea was an intense campaign that lasted almost throughout the whole Pacific War. There were two key places that defined the campaign. The first was the natural harbor on the island of Rabaul on the island of New Britain, north of New Guinea. The Japanese made this their strategic base in the region. The second was Port Moresby on the south coast of New Guinea.

Protecting Port Moresby

Japanese forces landed in New Guinea in March 1942. Their first attempt to take Port Moresby involved a naval operation. This was checked at the Battle of the Coral Sea in May 1942. The Japanese high command then decided to make a land assault south across the Owen Stanley mountains, following a route known as the Kokoda Trail. Air attacks on Port Moresby were supported by naval movements in Milne Bay, around the eastern tip of New Guinea. In September, Japanese troops reached to within 20 miles (30 km) of Port Moresby before being stopped.

An Allied counter offensive from November 1942 was met by stiff Japanese defense, but Japanese naval forces were defeated at the Battle of the Bismarck Sea in March 1943. Again, Japanese aircraft made attacks on Port Moresby, but in 1943 the tide had definitely turned. Allied forces began moving along the north coast, isolating Japanese strongpoints. The fighting on the island continued until 1945. The Japanese base at Rabaul held out until the end of the war.

KEY DATES

March 8, 1942 Japanese forces move into the Huon Peninsula on northeast New Guinea.

September 7, 1942 Japanese amphibious landings at Milne Bay are defeated.

September 17, 1942 Japanese forces are 20 miles (30 km) from Port Moresby on the southern coast of New Guinea.

January, 1943 Battle of Wau. Final major Japanese land offensive is stopped.

March, 1943 Japan loses eight transports and four destroyers as the Allies triumph at the Battle of the Bismarck Sea.

September 12, 1943 Allied forces take the key positions of Salamaua and Lae on the Gulf of Huon.

September 6, 1945 Allied forces finally enter Rabaul on New Britain.

1 Australian troops move forward through palm trees toward Japanese positions near Buna, supported by light tanks.

2 Japanese flags are displayed by weary U.S. troops after the Battle of Cape Gloucester, fought in 1944.

3 Humboldt Bay in New Guinea, April 1944. Landing craft head for the beach as the Allies move along the north coast.

4 U.S. troops advancing in the interior of the island of New Britain, towards Rabaul. There were few roads, and the tracks were difficult for vehicles to negotiate.

The Battle of Leyte Gulf

The October 1944 naval battle around the Philippine Islands—the largest naval battle of World War II—sealed the fate of the wartime Imperial Japanese Navy.

Corsairs armed with 500-pound (227 kg) bombs prepare to take off from a Central Pacific base.

TIMELINE **1944 SEPTEMBER–OCTOBER**

KEY: Pacific | Eastern Front | Europe and North Africa

September

September 2 Finland
Finland accepts a peace treaty with the Soviet Union and severs relations with Germany.

September 17 Holland
Operation Market Garden. The Allies suffer heavy losses as paratroopers try to seize key bridges.

September 22–25 Holland
Paratroopers retreat from Arnhem.

A kamikaze attacks the USS *Columbia* in January 1945, during U.S. landings in the Philippines.

The capture of the Marshall and the Mariana Islands brought U.S. forces to a position from which they could assault the Philippines. The first objective of General Douglas MacArthur was Leyte, an island in the southern Philippines. An amphibious assault would be supported by two naval fleets.

The Japanese plan to defend the islands was complex. A decoy force would draw the U.S. vessels away, while two attack forces would head for Leyte from the west and south. The plan would put nearly the whole Japanese navy into action. On October 23, 1944, U.S. submarines spotted the Japanese attack force and sank two cruisers. This was not a good start for the Japanese.

KEY DATES

October 20, 1944 U.S. forces land on eastern Leyte, in the Philippines.

October 22, 1944 Japan's decoy force and First Attack Force head for the Philippines.

October 23, 1944 U.S. submarines sink two Japanese cruisers and also severely damage a third.

October 24, 1944 Nearly 300 U.S. aircraft attack Kurita's force; Kurita withdraws to ambush U.S. carriers.

October 25, 1944 Japan's Force C are all but destroyed. Force A threatens the vulnerable U.S. landing fleet.

October 26, 1944 After a battle lasting 2 hours and 23 minutes, U.S. vessels defeat a larger Japanese force in another action at Leyte Gulf.

Continued on page 47

October

October 2 Poland
The last Poles in Warsaw surrender to the Germans; 150,000 Poles have died.

October 20 Philippines
The U.S. Sixth Army lands on Leyte Island in the Philippines; as he wades ashore, U.S. General Douglas MacArthur keeps a promise he made two years earlier: "I shall return."

October 23–26 Philippines
The Japanese Combined Fleet is defeated heavily at the Battle of Leyte Gulf. It loses 500 aircraft, 28 ships, and a submarine; U.S. losses are 200 aircraft and six ships.

Kamikaze

Meaning "divine wind," kamikaze were suicide pilots of the Japanese air force who flew their bomb-laden aircraft into U.S. ships. Japanese vice admiral Onishi said suicide missions were ideal for novice pilots: they just had to fly into the target. It was hard for U.S. antiaircraft gunners to destroy kamikaze planes in the air. Mass raids began over the Philippines in October 1944, reaching a peak off Okinawa between March and June 1945, when 1,475 suicide planes targeted U.S. ships in 10 separate attacks.

A Japanese raid on the U.S. Third Fleet sank the carrier *Princeton*. On October 24, U.S. aircraft sank the carrier *Musashi* and damaged the *Yamato*. The Japanese commander Takeo Kurita appeared to be on the retreat.

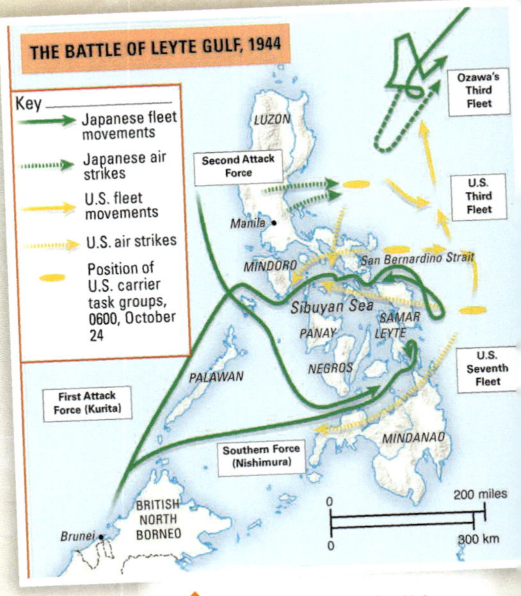

The battle began the U.S. reconquest of the Philippines.

Taking the Bait

Meanwhile, the U.S. Third Fleet had followed Japan's decoy force, leaving the Leyte landings exposed. Kurita turned around in the darkness and headed back toward Leyte. Japan's Force C and Second Attack Force were approaching through the Surigao Strait. The U.S. Seventh Fleet was vulnerable to a pincer movement. As Force C sailed down the strait, however, it was attacked by U.S. Task Group 77. The southern pincer collapsed.

TIMELINE 1944 NOVEMBER–DECEMBER

KEY: Pacific | Eastern Front | Europe and North Africa

November

November 7 Japan
The Japanese hang the spy Richard Sorge, a German newspaper correspondent who has been passing Japanese and German secrets to the Soviet Union.

November 11–12 Iwo Jima
U.S. warships bombard the Japanese-held island for the first time.

November 24 Japan
U.S. B-29 Superfortresses flying from the Mariana Islands raid Tokyo for the first time.

Kurita Withdraws

Kurita now moved against the weak U.S. landing fleet. Although he had a huge advantage in numbers of ships, his fuel was running low and he was anxious that U.S. backup might arrive. His battered force had had enough. He turned around and left Leyte.

A New Tactic

Leyte Gulf was a great U.S. victory. The crippling defeat marked the virtual end of Japan's Pacific threat. It also marked the first major use of kamikaze attacks. This tactic would become more common as the conflict in the Pacific went on.

October 1944. Led by the *Nagato*, Kurita's First Attack Force steams toward the Philippines.

Continued from page 45

November 1944 Japanese launch offensive on Leyte.

December 7, 1944 More U.S. troops land on Leyte.

December 15, 1944 U.S. troops land on Mindoro Island, southwest of Luzon.

January 9, 1945 U.S. Sixth Army lands at Lingayen Gulf in western Luzon.

March 3, 1945 Manila captured by U.S. troops after a month of fighting; the city is largely destroyed and 100,000 people are dead.

April 17, 1945 U.S. landings on Mindanao, the largest island in southern Philippines.

May 3, 1945 U.S. forces take the port of Davao with no resistance.

End June 1945 U.S. forces now control most of coast.

June 30, 1945 Despite pockets of Japanese resistance, Mindanao is in U.S. control.

December

December 4 Burma
The British Fourteenth Army begins the destruction of Japanese forces in Burma.

December 5–7 Philippines
U.S. forces begin a final offensive against Japanese lines on Leyte.

December 15 Philippines
The U.S. 24th Division lands on the island of Mindoro.

December 16 Belgium
Hitler begins Operation Watch on the Rhine, which aims to capture Antwerp. The Germans advance in thick fog. They are stopped by U.S. paratroopers in Bastogne.

War in Burma and China

Covering a huge area, the theaters of China and Burma posed acute logistics challenges.

1

In July 1937 Japanese forces undertook a full-scale invasion of China so beginning the Sino-Japanese War. Japan was initially successful, although the brutal nature of the campaign, including the so-called "Rape of Nanking," shocked the world. The Chinese government moved its capital west. Chinese forces undertook counter-offensives in 1939 and 1940, but the essential brake on the Japanese was the problem of supplying an army over the huge areas of China. It is estimated that over 20 million Chinese died during this war.

The Burma Campaign

From 1942 onward, campaigns in Burma were closely connected to the Sino-Japanese War because it was through Burma that aid was sent to the Chinese government. U.S. General Joseph Stilwell had the difficult task of trying to maintain the links to supply China using aircraft or by constructing an all-weather road through Burma.

Japanese forces occupied much of the British colony of Burma in 1942. In 1944, Japanese armies invaded India through northwestern Burma. This advance was defeated at the Battles of Imphal and Kohima, with the Japanese forces in full retreat by July 1944. The capital of Burma, Rangoon, was recaptured by the Allies in May 1945.

2

3

4

5

6

KEY DATES

July 7, 1937 The "Marco Polo Bridge Incident," the conflict used by Japanese forces as an excuse to begin a full-scale invasion of China.

August, 1941 U.S. aviator Claire Chennault's "Flying Tigers'" begin training to help China against Japan. Their first major action is against Japanese aircraft near the city of Kunming in December 1941.

1942 United States begins to send large-scale military aid to China.

February, 1942 Joseph Stilwell is placed in command of all U.S. forces in the China-India-Burma theatre.

July, 1942 British forces reach India after a long retreat through Burma.

August 21, 1944 Failure of the Japanese offensives against India from Burma.

1 Chiang Kai-shek, the Nationalist leader of China. He was unable to defeat the Japanese militarily but clung on to power.

2 General William Slim, who commanded the British 14th Army in Burma. He was a popular figure, known to his troops as "Bill."

3 Oil tanks burn as the British Army makes demolitions in Burma in 1942, during a retreat that covered hundreds of miles.

4 British forces move cautiously through a ruined temple as they take the offensive against the Japanese.

5 The fighting for Mandaly ended in victory for the Allies in 1945 as the Japanese were forced out.

6 Claire Lee Chennault, who helped the Nationalist Chinese by setting up the "Flying Tigers" to assist the Chinese air force.

Iwo Jima and Okinawa

By the end of 1944, U.S. forces were close to attacking Japan itself. They took part in two battles that would be among the hardest and most costly of the Pacific War.

U.S. troops unload supplies at Iwo Jima. Everything had to be shipped in, even fresh water.

TIMELINE **1945 JANUARY–FEBRUARY**

KEY:  **Pacific** **Eastern Front** **Europe and North Africa**

January

January 9 Philippines
Units of the U.S. Sixth Army make unopposed landings on the island of Luzon.

January 12–17 Poland
The Red Army begins its Vistula-Oder Offensive: two million men advance across the whole front.

January 27 Poland
The Red Army liberates the Nazi death camp at Auschwitz.

January 28 Belgium
The German Ardennes Offensive has cost about 100,000 German lives, with about 81,000 U.S. casualties.

January 30 Germany
Soviet forces reach the Oder River, only 100 miles (160 km) from Berlin.

Iwo Jima's three airfields were useful bases from which to attack Japan.

The final drive that would bring U.S. forces within range of the Japanese home islands depended on the capture of Iwo Jima and Okinawa.

KEY DATES

February 17, 1945 U.S. Marines land on southwest coast of Iwo Jima.

February 23, 1945 U.S. forces reach summit of Mt. Suribachi.

March 16, 1945 Iwo Jima declared secure.

April 1, 1945 U.S. troops land on Okinawa.

April 4, 1945 U.S. troops on Okinawa reach Machinato Line.

April 28, 1945 U.S. forces reach second defensive line.

June 22, 1945 U.S. troops finally take Okinawa.

Iwo Jima

The volcanic island of Iwo Jima was a natural fortress defended by 21,000 Japanese. Major General Kuribayashi had built a defensive complex with miles of tunnels and trenches. He intended that his troops would take cover and lure U.S. troops inland.

In the shadow of Mt. Suribachi, U.S. Marines take cover on a beach of black volcanic sand on Iwo Jima, March 5, 1945.

February

February 3 Philippines
U.S. forces enter Manila, capital of the Philippines; Japanese forces virtually destroy the city in a month's fighting known as the "Rape of Manila."

February 4 Soviet Union
Stalin, Roosevelt, and Churchill meet at Yalta to decide the division of postwar Europe.

February 13–14 Germany
British bombers bomb Dresden, creating a firestorm that kills at least 50,000 people.

February 14 Germany
As the Red Army advances, half of the 2.3 million population of German East Prussia flees west. Thousands die from cold or exhaustion.

February 17 Iwo Jima
U.S. Marines land on the island of Iwo Jima, which they capture after a month of heavy fighting.

Antiaircraft Fire

During the Pacific War, the number of antiaircraft guns mounted on U.S. warships steadily increased. As early as May 1942 it became clear that aircraft, and not heavy guns, would be the main threat to naval vessels. Early on in the war, an American battleship carried few antiaircraft guns. By the time the U.S. Pacific Fleet was fighting off kinawa, the number of guns had risen. The kamikaze attacks made the need for antiaircraft fire even more important as the Japanese used every means to attack ships.

→ A warship fires rockets as a U.S. landing craft approaches Okinawa.

The U.S. Invasion

Preparations for Operation Detachment began in June 1944, when U.S. bombers attacked Iwo Jima. Beginning on December 8, U.S. forces bombed Iwo Jima every day for 72 days in the longest aerial bombing of the Pacific War. Two divisions of U.S. Marines landed on the beaches of Iwo Jima on February 17. The island was declared secure after nearly four weeks of fighting that took a high toll on both sides. Of the Japanese defenders, nearly 20,000 died.

The Battle for Okinawa

The next U.S. target was Okinawa in the Ryukyu group of islands, between Kyushu, the most southerly of Japan's home islands, and Formosa (Taiwan). U.S. and British carrier aircraft attacked airfields on Kyushu and Formosa to isolate Okinawa from March 1944. In the last week of March, Okinawa itself came under heavy

TIMELINE **1945 MARCH–APRIL**

KEY: Pacific | Eastern Front | Europe and North Africa

March

March 7 Japan
A U.S. bombing raid on Tokyo kills 83,000 people and destroys a large area of the city.

March 16 Iwo Jima
The Americans declare the island secure. They have lost 6,821 soldiers and sailors; of the 21,000 Japanese defenders, nearly 20,000 are dead.

March 23 Germany
British and U.S. forces start to cross the Rhine River. German troops offer little resistance.

April

April 1 Okinawa
Some 183,000 men of the U.S. Tenth Army land on the island, which is only 325 miles (520 km) from Japan.

April 7 Pacific Ocean
U.S. bombers on their way to Okinawa sink the *Yamato*, the world's largest battleship.

Japanese prisoners wait to be questioned on Okinawa on June 21.

naval bombardment and air attack.

The landings began on April 1, with around 182,000 U.S. troops supported by an armada of warships. At sea, Japanese kamikaze pilots flew some 2,000 sorties, sinking 21 warships. It took until June 22 to declare Okinawa secure. Some 100,000 Japanese defenders died, along with about 12,000 Americans.

Okinawa had higher Allied casualties than any other Pacific War campaign. The losses made U.S. planners fearful of the casualties that would result from an invasion of Japan itself.

U.S. Marine Corps

The Marines who led the Iwo Jima and Okinawa landings were amphibious soldiers of the U.S. Navy. During the war, the Marine Corps suffered heavy losses because they were involved in the fiercest fighting. Admiral Chester Nimitz wrote, "Among the Americans who served on Iwo Jima, uncommon valor was a common virtue."

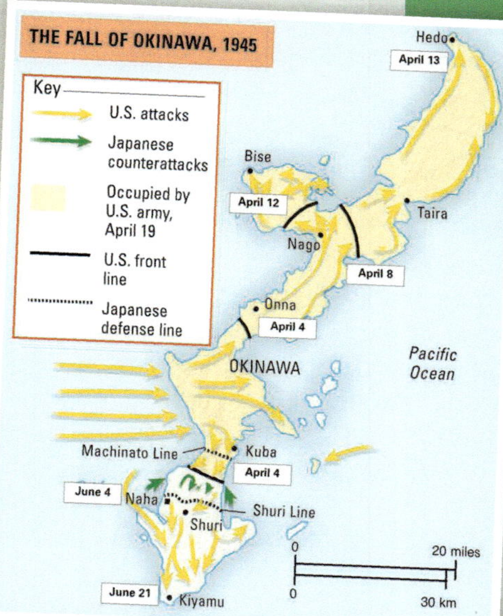

Map of the fighting on Okinawa. U.S. troops faced stiff resistance from the Japanese.

April 12 United States
President Roosevelt dies of a brain hemorrhage; Vice President Harry S. Truman takes over as president.

April 16 Germany
The Soviets attack Berlin; they vastly outnumber the Germans in troops, tanks, weapons, and aircraft.

April 28 Italy
Mussolini is shot dead by partisans as he tries to flee to Austria.

April 29 Italy
German forces in northern Italy surrender to the Allies.

April 30 Germany
Hitler and Eva Braun commit suicide in their bunker in Berlin.

Soviets Invade Manchuria

The most successful Blitzkrieg campaign of World War II was the Soviet invasion of Manchuria in 1945.

One of the strangest aspects of World War II was that Japan and the Soviet Union were not at war until the final days of the conflict. Their forces faced each other across common borders in Manchuria, but in 1941 the Japanese decided not to attack the Soviets. They believed that Russia would soon fall to Hitler and that Japanese resources were better employed in the Pacific region.

The Timetable Is Set

For his part, Joseph Stalin needed all the troops he could assemble to meet the German threat in the west, and he was only too happy to be able to move troops from the Russian Far East to Europe late in 1941. Stalin was encouraged in this by reports from a spy, Richard Sorge, who had access to Japanese plans. Soviet troops from the Far East led the offensive that saw the withdrawal of Germans from Moscow in December 1941.

In 1943, Stalin agreed that the Soviet Union would go to war with Japan after Germany had been defeated. The Allied focus was now on the consequences of an invasion of Japan. The power of the atomic bomb was not yet known, and the invasion of Japan was expected to involve huge loss of life for American troops.

Stalin attacked Manchuria on August 9, 1945, precisely three months after the end of the European war as he had agreed. This astonishingly successful "Blitzkrieg" swept through to the Pacific coast in days. It ended with Soviet troops in the Korean peninsula and set the scene for the establishment of communist states in China and North Korea, which would have profound consequences for the world.

KEY DATES

November, 1943 At the Tehran Conference between Allied leaders, Stalin agrees to attack Japan after the war in Europe has ended. This agreement is confirmed at the Yalta Conference of February 1945.

June, 1945 Final U.S. victory on Okinawa. Japanese losses are 100,000 killed on Okinawa, the first of the home islands to be invaded by U.S. forces. Just 7,000 Japanese regular troops are taken prisoner. It is estimated that any successful invasion of Japan would result in over one million Japanese casualties.

August 9, 1942 Red Army invades Manchuria.

August 18, 1942 Soviet troops make amphibious landings in Korea.

August 20, 1942 Soviet troops stop at the 38th Parallel in Korea.

1 Aleksandr Mikhaylovich Vasilevsky. He was the key planner in the Manchurian campaign as Red Army chief of staff.

2 Vasilevsky and other senior Soviet officers land in Port Arthur in order to formally accept the Japanese surrender.

3 Chairman Mao reads out the declaration of the Communist People's Republic of China in Beijing in 1949.

4 August 9, 1945. Soviet infantry cross the border into Manchuria, beginning their advance to the Pacific coast.

The Surrender of Japan

As their forces neared Japan, U.S. military planners faced a dilemma. Any invasion would likely cause huge casualties, among both troops and civilians.

Months after the blast, Hiroshima lies in ruins; about 4.5 square miles (11.65 sq km) of the city was flattened.

TIMELINE 1945 MAY–JUNE

KEY: Pacific | Eastern Front | Europe and North Africa

May

May 2 Germany
The Reichstag falls to the Red Army after a savage three-day battle.

May 3 Burma
Rangoon falls to the Allies without a fight after 38 months of Japanese occupation.

May 8 Europe
Victory in Europe (VE) Day; the Allies accept the German surrender.

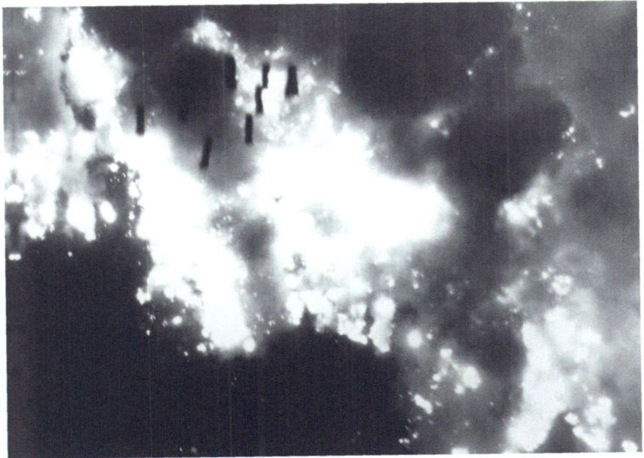

Fires blazing in Takamatsu port silhouette bombs dropped from a B-29 flying at high altitude.

KEY DATES

July 16, 1945 Manhattan Project successfully tests the world's first atomic bomb at Alamogordo, New Mexico.

August 6, 1945 United States drops an atomic bomb on Hiroshima, Japan.

August 9, 1945 Soviet Union declares war on Japan.

August 9, 1945 United States drops a second atomic bomb on Nagasaki; the Soviet Red Army invades Manchuria to fight the Japanese Imperial Army.

August 10, 1945 Emperor Hirohito and Foreign Minister Shigenori Togo convince the Japanese military to accept defeat.

August 15, 1945 A cease-fire comes into effect.

September 2, 1945 Japan signs the formal surrender on the battleship USS *Missouri* in Tokyo Bay.

Both the United States and Japan were planning for a U.S. invasion of Japan. Based on Japanese resistance elsewhere in the Pacific, U.S. commanders feared that the invasion would be the most bloody encounter of the war.

Japan's Defensive Preparations

In April 1945, the Japanese launched Operation Ketsu-go for two million soldiers to defend the four home islands and Korea. They increased their ground forces with the People's Volunteer Combat Corps, a home guard organization. Propaganda called for the country's defenders to fight to the end rather than endure the humiliation of living under U.S. occupation.

June

June 1 Burma
British troops are mopping up the 700,000 Japanese left scattered widely around Burma.

June 22 Okinawa
Japanese resistance ends on Okinawa; the battle costs the Japanese 100,000 dead, including some 26,000 civilians, many of whom choose to commit suicide.

The Tokyo Fire Raids

The first great incendiary raid on Tokyo was on the night of March 9-10, 1945, when 279 B-29s dropped 2,000 tons of bombs. The resulting fires destroyed 25 percent of Tokyo's buildings, killed 83,000 people, injured 41,000, and left one million homeless. The B-29s returned twice more. Just three raids destroyed more than half the city, an area covering some 50 square miles (129 sq km).

→ Dust sucked in by the blast at ground level forms a mushroom cloud above Nagasaki.

Bombing Campaign

In early 1945, U.S. bombers began dropping incendiary bombs to start fires. The first raid used the new tactic on the night of March 9–10, 1945, on Tokyo. It devastated the city. After the capture of airfields on Iwo Jima, bombers expanded their operations to include daylight raids with high-explosive bombs. By May, U.S. fighters had air superiority above Japan. Bombers flattened much of Japan's six major industrial centers: Kawasaki, Kobe, Nagoya, Osaka, Tokyo, and Yokahama.

Japanese Morale

The morale of Japanese civilians began to crumble as food and shelter grew scarce, and the infrastructure collapsed. Emperor Hirohito wanted to surrender, but the military refused.

→ "Little Boy," the atomic bomb used at Hiroshima, had the power of 15,000 tons of conventional explosives.

TIMELINE **1945 JULY–SEPTEMBER**

KEY:  Pacific | Eastern Front | Europe and North Africa

July 17–August 2 Germany
President Harry S. Truman, Stalin, and new British Prime Minister Clement Attlee meet at Potsdam to discuss postwar policy in Europe.

July

August

August 6 Japan
A B-29 Superfortress drops an atomic bomb on the Japanese city of Hiroshima, killing 70,000 and injuring a similar number.

August 9 Manchuria
A huge Soviet offensive begins against the Japanese Kwantung Army.

August 9 Japan
Atomic bomb dropped on Nagasaki, killing 35,000 people. The Japanese decide to surrender.

A New Weapon

Meanwhile, after years of secret research, the United States had tested the first atomic bomb. The new president, Harry S. Truman, decided to use it against Japan rather than risk an invasion. The first atomic bomb was dropped on August 6 on Hiroshima, a city of 245,000 people. Two-thirds of the city was destroyed. When no Japanese surrender came, a second bomb was dropped on Nagasaki on August 9. Meanwhile, the Soviet Red Army attacked Japanese troops in China.

The Japanese Surrender

The Japanese military was forced to accept defeat. On August 15, a cease-fire came into effect. Hirohito spoke on the radio to tell the Japanese people that they must "bear the unbearable." The war in the Pacific was over.

Emperor Hirohito's Broadcast

At noon on August 15, 1945, Emperor Hirohito made a radio broadcast. He told his people that it was his and their painful duty to surrender without further bloodshed. Hirohito had godlike status in Japan. He had never spoken directly to his people. His speech helped the transition from war to peace go more smoothly than some observers had feared.

Crew on USS *Missouri* watch the formal Japanese surrender taking place on September 2, 1945.

August 15 Japan
Victory over Japan (VJ) Day; the Japanese surrender is announced to a grateful Allied public.

August 16 Manchuria
The Soviet campaign against the Japanese ends in total victory. Soviet troops enter Korea.

September

September 2 Japan
Aboard the U.S. battleship *Missouri* in Tokyo Bay, Japanese officials sign the Instrument of Surrender; World War II is finally over.

Aftermath of the War

The War in the Pacific changed the political landscape of East Asia and led to the independence of former colonies.

General Douglas MacArthur signed the treaty whereby Japan surrendered unconditionally on board USS *Missouri* in Tokyo Bay on 2 September 1945. Japan was a country in ruins: all major cities had been bombed by U.S. aircraft and two of them, Hiroshima and Nagasaki, had been pulverized by atomic bombs. Japan was occupied by U.S. forces and the Japanese political system underwent great changes, but Emperor Hirohito remained the head of state.

Communism in Asia

Elsewhere in Asia, the war had profound effects. In northeast Asia, the arrival of Soviet forces in Manchuria and Korea gave a boost to local communist parties. Korea was divided and North Korea became a communist state. In China the communists, led by Mao Zhedong, began a civil war that resulted in the defeat of the Nationalist government of Chiang Kai-shek.

Much of south and southeast Asia had been colonies of European powers before 1941. This changed rapidly after the war. Dutch colonies fought a war of independence and became the nation of Indonesia in 1949. In 1947, the British Raj in India was divided into the new states of India and Pakistan. In southeast Asia, Burma became independent of British rule. In what are now Vietnam, Cambodia, and Laos, France tried to retain control. In Vietnam this led to a long war with communist nationalists that eventually involved the United States during the 1960s.

KEY DATES

August, 1945 Nationalists in the Dutch East Indies proclaim independence from Holland. After a bitter war, the country becomes independent in 1949.

December, 1946 Fighting begins between the Viet Minh and French forces in Vietnam.

August 15, 1947 British India becomes the two independent nations of India and Pakistan.

October 1, 1949 Mao Zhedong proclaims communist rule in China.

April, 1952 San Francisco Treaty comes into force, and Allied occupation of Japan ends.

1 The ruins of Hiroshima, destroyed by a single atomic bomb dropped from the B-29 Superfortress named "Enola Gay."

2 Douglas MacArthur with Emperor Hirohito. MacArthur helped to change the Japanese political system.

3 U.S. troops man a howitzer on the Kum River during the Korean War, when communist North Korea invaded the South.

4 The crew of a U.S. M24 tank during the early stages of the Korean War, holding the line against the invading North.

5 French prisoners march into captivity after their defeat at Dien Bien Phu in 1954, which ended French control of Vietnam.

Glossary

amphibious assaults An attack by soldiers who land from the sea.

atoll A coral island of a reef surrounding a lagoon.

atomic bomb An explosive device that creates huge power by splitting or fusing atoms.

battleship The largest and most heavily armored type of warship.

convoy A number of ships or vehicles traveling together.

corps A military unit made up of several divisions.

counterattack An attack by a defending force.

decoy Something used to lure the enemy into a trap.

evacuation The removal of people from a dangerous area.

garrison A military base.

incendiary A bomb that is designed to start fires.

infrastructure The roads, railroads, supplies, and organization that allow a community to function.

intelligence Information learned from secret services or code breakers.

kamikaze A Japanese suicide pilot.

marine A soldier based on a ship who fights on land.

morale The emotional well-being of people.

neutralize To make sure that an enemy force has no effect on the conflict.

occupation Military control of part of a country by forces from another.

peninsula An area of land that juts into water.

retaliation Revenge for a previous event.

strait A short, narrow stretch of water between two bodies of land.

strategic Useful in achieving a long-term goal.

strategy A long-term plan of action.

surrender To stop fighting and give in to the enemy.

Further Resources

Books

Ellis, Catherine. *Key Figures of World War II*. Rosen Publishing, 2016.

Hardyman, Robyn. *What Caused World War II? (Why Wars Happened)*. Gareth Stevens, 2017.

Harriot, Emma. *Did Anything Good Come Out of World War II?* Rosen Publishing, 2016.

Hunter, Nick. *World War II (Frontline Soldiers and Their Families)*. Gareth Stevens, 2016.

Lyons, Michael J., and David J. Ulbrich. *World War II, A Global History*. Routledge, 2021.

National Geographic. *Everything World War II*. National Geographic Kids, 2021.

Owens, Lisa L. *World War II Code Breakers*. Lerner Publishing Group, 2019.

Owens, Lisa L. *Attack on Pearl Harbor*. Lerner Publications, 2018.

Smithsonian Museum. *World War II Map by Map*. Dorling Kindersley, 2019.

Smithsonian Museum. *World War II The Definitive Visual History*. Dorling Kindersley, 2015.

Stille, Mark E. *The United States Navy in World War II*. Osprey, 2021.

Websites

americanhistory.si.edu/price-of-freedom
A site that covers all U.S. military history from the 18th century.

www.nationalww2museum.org/war/articles/pacific-strategy-1941-1944
Explanation of the Pacific Strategy from the National WWII Museum, New Orleans. Including maps and other links.

www.ibiblio.org/pha
A collection of primary World War II source materials.

education.nationalgeographic.org/resource/world-war-ii-pacific
Click through the National Geographic timelins of World War II in the Pacific.

war-experience.org/wwii-timeline/
The Second World War Experience Center.

Index